The Hammock

★ A CELEBRATION OF A SUMMER CLASSIC ★

DANIEL MACK

STEWART, TABORI & CHANG NEW YORK

The gifts of the hammock are many.

It protects, it cools, it's portable,

but most importantly, it relaxes.

4 ★

It is not first and foremost a place to eat or drink

or even read a book.

In its essence, it is a place to enjoy solitude.

There is hardly a family photo album missing the idyllic hammock.

In fact, there are many early tintypes of people in hammocks.

The frugal traveler in equatorial areas knows the hammock well.

It is everywhere.

You can rent one, buy one, or just hook up your own.

You see them in lightly sheltered hammock huts, and on boats.

8 ★

Hammocks help turn backyards into living areas.

A hammock is the ideal place for a quick rest—or a long nap.

They were readily available

in catalogs and general stores

at the start of the twentieth century.

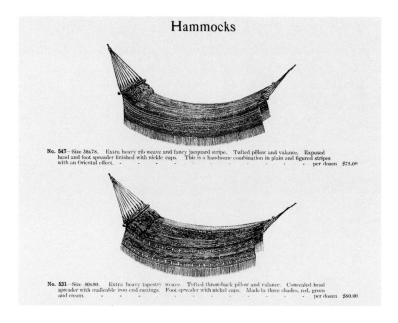

Hammocks

No. 547—Size 38x78. Extra heavy rib weave and fancy jacquard stripe. Tufted pillow and valance. Exposed head and foot spreader finished with nickle caps. This is a handsome combination in plain and figured stripes with an Oriental effect. - per dozen $75.00

No. 531—Size 40x80. Extra heavy tapestry weave. Tufted throw-back pillow and valance. Concealed head spreader with malleable iron end castings. Foot spreader with nickel caps. Made in three shades, red, green and cream. - - - - - - - - - - - - - - - - - - - per dozen $80.00

OUR LINE OF HAMMOCKS.

WHEN HANGING A HAMMOCK ALWAYS HANG IT SO THAT HEAD WILL BE HIGHER THAN THE FOOT.

The most select line of Hammocks ever placed on the market. We have selected this line of Hammocks with a view to giving our customers the best possible value for their money.
SEE OUR PRICES.

Mexican Woven Hammock, 80 Cents.

No. 6R7231 Mexican Woven Hammock, made of sisal twine, fancy assorted colors. Entire length, 12 feet 6 inches; length of bed, 6 feet. Rope edge. Weight, 3 lbs. Price, without spreaders, each.....80c

Canvas Hammocks. No. 6R7234

This is the latest thing in Hammocks. These hammocks are made of canvas throughout, are very strong and durable, and we predict a large sale for them. They are made of 8-ounce canvas and surely become popular. The bed is about 7 feet long and 3 feet wide, and they are similar to hammocks used in the U.S. Navy. All have spreaders at each end.
No. 6R7232 Made of 8-ounce canvas, spreader at each end, without valance. Price, each........85c
No. 6R7233½ Made of striped canvas, fancy stripes, spreader at each end, without valance. Price, each............................$1.10
No. 6R7234 Made of striped canvas, fancy stripes, spreader at each end, with valance. Price, each............................$1.40

Weight, 4 pounds.

Open Weave Cotton Hammocks, 55c.

No. 6R7235 Open Weave Cotton Hammocks. Fine cotton weave, quarter colors with fancy colored stripes. Size of bed, 6¼ feet long, 3 feet wide. Strong and durable; without pillow or spreader. A good hammock for children. Weight, 5 pounds.
Our special price...............................55c

Cotton Weave Hammock with Pillow and Spreader, 85 Cents.

No. 6R7237 Cotton Hammock, with close woven body, of the best cotton weave, full fancy colors, with spreader and pillow. Size of bed, 6¼ feet long, 3 feet wide. A hammock that sells regularly at $1.25 to $1.50. Weight, 3¼ pounds. Our special price, with fancy pillow and spreader..........................85c

Canvas Weave Hammock with Pillow and Spreader, $1.25.

No. 6R7239 Hammock. Made of closest fancy canvas weave, in full fancy bright colors. Made with three-ply warps, with fancy colored pillow and spreader. A very strong hammock. Retails from $1.75 to $2.00. Size of bed, 6¼ feet long, 3 feet wide. Weight, 4 lbs. Our special price...$1.25

Special Value with Fringe Valance at $1.15.

No. 6R7241 Cotton Hammock, close excelsior weave, with short fancy fringe valance; full fancy bright colors; with pillow and spreader. Size of bed, 6¼ feet long, 3 feet wide. A first class hammock in every respect. Sells regularly at $1.50. Weight, 5 pounds. Our special price...........$1.15

Our Leader $2.25 Value for $1.50.

No. 6R7242 Hammocks, fine excelsior weave with deep woven valance with fringe, full fancy bright colors, with one spreader and one pillow. Size of bed, 6¼ feet long, 3 feet wide. A beauty for the money. Weight, about 4½ lbs. Our special price, $1.50

Our Damask Weave Hammock, $2.05.

No. 6R7243 Our Big Leader Hammock, made in figured fancy weave, damask pattern, full fancy fluted valance, with fringe and scroll pattern. One strong spreader at head, with fancy pillow, also one short wood spreader at the foot. Size of bed, 40x80 inches. One of the most beautiful hammocks ever placed on the market. Strong and durable, and one which generally sells at retail for $3.00. Weight, 6¼ pounds. Our special price.........$2.05

Our Canvas Weave Hammock, $2.75.

No. 6R7245 Hammock, extra heavy, fancy close canvas weave, fine fancy bright colors, extra deep fluted valance with fancy tufted pillow, heavy strong spreader. One short wood bar at the foot. Size of bed, 40x84 inches. This is a large size hammock, strong, durable and very showy. Weight, 9 pounds. Our special price............................$2.75

Our Damask Pattern Tufted Pillow Hammock, $2.55.

No. 6R7248 Our Large Size, Tufted Pillow Hammock. This hammock is made in full fancy colors, strong spreader and detachable, tufted pillow at one end with extra wood bar as shown in the illustration, full deep valance at the sides. Size of bed, 40x82 inches. The pillow is made so that it can be easily detached if not desired, and we consider this one of the best bargains which we offer in hammocks. Weight, 10 pounds.
Our special price for this full size hammock, $2.55

Close Woven Baby or Child's Hammock, 50 Cents.

No. 6R7255 Child's Hammock, cotton cord open mesh. Entire length from end to end, 6 feet 6 inches; bed 4½ feet long. Strong, well made and durable; just the thing for the baby. Weight, 16 ounces.
Price, each...50c

Our Portable Swinging Hammock Chair, 85 Cents.

This Chair is so constructed that it may be hung on a porch, under a tree, in the orchard, lawn, in fact can be hung almost anywhere, and may be used as a chair or a hammock.

This portable chair is made of a wood frame, with awning drilling fabric to serve as a seat or back. It is 45 inches long, 25 inches wide, and weighs about 7 pounds. It is adjusted to different positions by drawing in or letting out ropes and tieing knot when in the position desired.
No. 6R7258 Our special price on this Portable Hammock Chair, only.......................85c

---

Hammock Hooks.

No. 6R7266 Screw Hammock Hooks, tinned, 7/16-inch diameter, to screw in.
Price, each..5c
If by mail, postage extra, 3 cents.

No. 6R7267 Plate Hammock Hooks, tinned, 7/16-inch in diameter to fasten with screws. Price, each........................6c
If by mail, postage extra, 3 cents.

LAWN SWINGS, $3.50 and $4.25
For Children and Adults

This is the best Lawn Swing on the market. It is made of hard pine and gum wood, with connections well bolted and well braced, painted in red color, and after they are started the swinging is continued by pressing the feet on the foot-board. It is great fun for the children, and adults will find them quite comfortable.
No. 6R7271 Adult's size, about 8½ feet high. The seat is 30 inches wide, which is wider than the ordinary chair and will hold two grown persons or four children. Weight, about 100 lbs. Price, each..$3.50
No. 6R7272 Large size, 10 feet high, seat 30 inches wide, large enough to seat four adults or six children. Weight, about 150 pounds. Price, each........$4.25
We can furnish larger swings to special order for public amusements, such as picnic groves, etc., from 8 to 16 feet high, made extra strong for rough use, if wanted.

Our Acme Folding Lawn Settee, 86c.

No. 6R7274 For 86 cents we offer you our Acme Lawn Settee, made of selected wood, painted in a bright attractive color and constructed on substantial principles. This lawn settee is made so it may be folded up and set away during the winter or it may be left on a porch as desired. The acme lawn settee is a very useful and desirable article and will recommend itself to our customers, in fact it requires no care or attention and saves many times its value in the wear and tear of regular household furniture. Our acme lawn settee, 3½ feet long, painted. Weight, 20 pounds. At our special price..........................86c

The Chicago Folding Porch Chair.

No. 6R7278 The Chicago Folding Porch Chair. All joints riveted and may be folded when not in use. Weighs about 10½ pounds and the back may be adjusted to various angles for comfort. All have arm rests and high back are easily carried about and saves the household furniture.
Price, each. . ..84c

REPAIR PARTS FOR FLOBERT RIFLES.

NOTICE—These parts are not fitted. They are in a filed state and must be fitted by a gunsmith or mechanic. If possible send us the broken part and we will try to match it as near as we can.

Flobert Breech Blocks.
No. 6R7300 Remington Action Breech Blocks, filed, cut nose.
Price, each...........25c
No. 6R7301 Remington Action Breech Blocks, filed, pointed nose.
Price, each...........25c
If by mail, postage extra, 2 cents.

Warrant Breech Blocks.
No. 6R7303 For light Warrant action Floberts, weighing about 4½ pounds, not fitted. Each.35c
No. 6R7304 For heavy Warrant Floberts, weighing about 6 pounds, not fitted. Price, each.............35c
If by mail, postage extra, 6 cents.

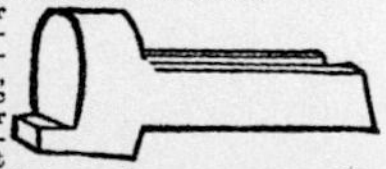

Improved Warrant Breech Blocks.
No. 6R7305 For light improved Warrant action, like our No. 6R858, not finished.
Price, each.........40c
No. 6R7306 For heavy improved Warrant action, like our No. 6R659 or No. 6R663, not finished.
Price, each.............40c
If by mail, postage extra, 5 cents.

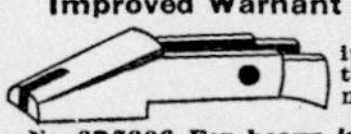

★ 15

Each handwoven hammock
is a work of art.

Hammocks should be washed
each fall,
left to dry in the sun,
and hung in a sheltered place
until winter passes.
And they, in return
for your care,
will provide a quiet place
to rest for a decade of summers.

There are great powers folded into the simple hammock.

Its simplicity hides its versatility.

It allows. It allows fleetness and relaxation.

It reminds.

It reminds us that there are times and places,

rhythms and ways of being

that are not easily reached but always there.

It waits.

It waits for us to slow down, breathe differently, think differently, feel differently.

It's a hideaway,

a refuge where, as you unwind,

loosen up, unbend,

other things start to happen.

A thought or two drifts in

from who knows where.

You might notice

the light of the day

or smell something that is only

present when you are still.

There may be a noise, a bird,

a bug, or just the movement

of the wind in the trees.

★ 25

Sometimes it's all in a glance or a look.

Children seem to know more about hammocks than adults.

There's an air of easy repose, joy, and something, well, ancient.

The hammock resembles a kind of womb . . .

. . . cradling young and old alike.

Almost any creature can appreciate its allure.

Our admiration for the hammock is so great,

we've even begun making them for our pets.

Relaxing is a brave, radical activity.

    It boldly celebrates the importance of idleness, calmness, inactivity, stillness.

Lying in a hammock is an experiment in the imagination.

    The imagination, in some people's view, is the sixth sense.

It allows us to perceive and feel things

    just beyond the reach of our other senses.

| Introduction

It is a visitor from another time and place. It beckons, invites, holds, rocks, lulls, and sometimes dumps us unceremoniously on the ground. It was "discovered" by Columbus, but it had lifetimes of use before then. The hammock quickly improved the quality of life for armies and navies around the world. Inventors have tinkered with and elaborated it over and over. The hammock is hiding in plain sight—and its meanings are many. Here's a quick journey back in time.

It does day in and day out work in many developing countries and is, itself, the livelihood

The hammock soothes, gently shaping to the body's natural curvature.

It allows the back to align, the muscles to relax,

and the stresses of everyday life to slip away.

8 Côte d'Ivoire - ABENGOUROU - Le Roi dans son hamac

of many people. Competition is now heating up between Mexican makers, for whom the hammock is both a traditional cultural object and a cottage industry, and newly arrived makers of hammocks in China. Almost half a million are sold each year around the world and it is estimated that more than 27 million people sleep in hammocks each night in Central and South America alone, although that number is diminishing as air conditioners make the ventilation provided by the hammock less necessary.

Some people know it through traveling or camping, and since it first appeared, artists and writers have added it to their work. Sculptors and furniture makers have admired its shape and motion.

This book is a collection of the many intertwined and yet sometimes conflicting lives of the simple hammock. It is as beautiful and intricate a story as the colored cotton strings from which so many are woven.

Today, we best know the hammock as that part of the backyard where we too rarely spend time. It waits and we appreciate it.

For young and old, stringing up the backyard hammock

marks the beginning of another summer.

And yet, there is something at once alluring and repelling about a hammock. The promise of rest and perhaps sleep is comforting. But for those of us in the post-industrial world there is something a bit indolent about the hammock as well.

A hammock is temporary, soft, portable, personal, protective, soothing, cheap, and sometimes easy to make—whether from a big piece of canvas or a woven rope or a delicate mesh of colored threads. These are remarkable features when you consider them. And they have led this simple object to a wide variety of uses around the world.

It's likely that the hammock started or doubled as a fishing net, the kind that is thrown into the water and hauled back in. They are strong and relatively lightweight. Was there that "aha" moment somewhere, sometime, when, as a fishing net was laid out to dry, someone thought: "I think I'll just rest here in this net for a few minutes"?

THE HAMMOCK

BY LI-YOUNG LEE

When I lay my head in my mother's lap
I think how day hides the star,
the way I lay hidden once, waiting
inside my mother's singing to herself. And I remember
how she carried me on her back
between home and the kindergarten,
once each morning and once each afternoon.

I don't know what my mother's thinking.

When my son lays his head in my lap, I wonder:
Do his father's kisses keep his father's worries
from becoming his? I think, Dear God, and remember
there are stars we haven't heard from yet:
They have so far to arrive. Amen,
I think, and I feel almost comforted.

I've no idea what my child is thinking

Between two unknowns, I live my life.
Between my mother's hopes, older than I am
by coming before me. And my child's wishes, older than I am
by outliving me. And what's it like?
Is it a door, and a good-bye on either side?
A window and eternity on either side?
Yes, and a little singing between two great rests.

| # History Entwined

The hammock is a witness, a memento, and an unknowing link to the rich history of European presence in the Americas. It was one of the exotic discoveries that Columbus brought back from his first voyage to what he thought, and always thought, was Asia. It joined tobacco, pineapple, avocado, the canoe, barbecued meat, and, of course, gold as the booty and the motivation for Spain, Portugal, Britain, the Netherlands, and France to explore the Americas. Each trip back was more costly for the native peoples.

Fernández de Oviedo y Valdés came to America in 1514, where for more than thirty years he compiled detailed ethnographic descriptions of the myriad of goods, products,

The white fringe on many hammocks is said to keep bugs away.

peoples, and customs of the Caribbean and Central America.

Adapting the Hammock

In *La Historia General y Natural de las Indias* (1535), Oviedo writes:

> The indians sleep in a bed they call an 'hamaca' which looks like a piece of cloth with both an open and tight weave, like a net . . . made of cotton . . . about 2.5 or 3 yards long, with many henequen twine strings at either end which can be hung at any height. They are good beds, and clean . . . and since the weather is warm they require no covers at all . . . and they are portable so a child can carry it over the arm.

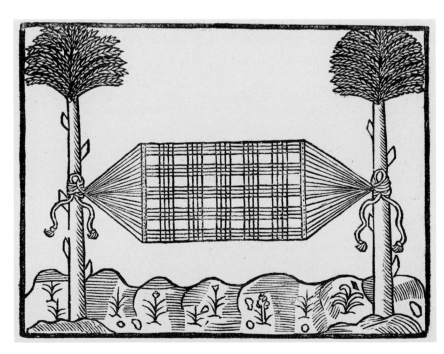

These early hammocks were varied. Some were made from cotton; others blended a rope or cord made from the barks or fibers of trees or local plants: henequen sisal, jute. Others were made from the tough, long leaves of trees like banana or palm. Since the hammock is so perfectly simple, it's likely that early hammocks resembled ones still in use today in various Central and South American tribes.

THE TRIBAL HAMMOCK

The lightweight, versatile, and inexpensive hammock is a vital item in many cultures. To tribal and indigenous peoples, the hammock is an important item among usually very few household goods. There are perhaps some stools, cooking and eating utensils, and the versatile hammock—part bed, chair, and cradle. Even a big one weighs only about five pounds, so it is easy to move around.

CANTICLE OF THE HAMMOCK

R. FREIRE RIBEIRO, TRANSLATION BY JAMES BOGAN

On the old plantations in the lands of the North
that's where you would find pretty hammocks
with intricate fringes the color of the moon . . .
I remember my grandfather, remembering the girls of Recife.
I can see him still, stretched out in the hammock
his large feet bare, his head turned to the past.
And I remember his mother,
Sonia, she was the little oldie,
seated in the hammock, talking alone
with eyes full of shades from beyond.
Actually she was a poor thing,
perched in the hammock
that comes and goes
vaivem vaivem
that comes and goes

In the shacks by the road
in the palaces of the rich
innocent children swing in the hammock.
A mother lulls the swaying child
with songs smooth, soft, and gentle.
She imagines these songs sung
by birds in the kingdom of Heaven.

Even on a long road comes sweet rest
for soldiers of the infantry.
Then they lay in their grey hammocks
reposed after the long day's march
suspended amongst the crowded trees
watching the stars, lost in the sky.

And is not the hammock a proper vessel for the dead?

The dead one looks asleep
dreaming a dream of emptiness
echoing with the cries of the living.
Carried by two friends
the body rocks to the rhythm of their walk.
Carried by two friends
the body swings until it comes to rest
in the depths of the ground.
Ah, the new moon is a silver hammock
shining in our sky suspended on the deep.
"God rests in this moon," old Sonia says.
Does He rest in the beautiful floating moon
watching from afar the sorrows of his distant children?

★ 49

This drawing was part of the book La Historia General y Natural de las Indias *published in 1535.*

BIRTH AND DEATH IN HAMMOCKS

The hammock has often been involved in birthing. It is still used in many Latin countries. A woman may use the hammock for support as she is squatting to give birth or she may be lying in the hammock and give birth through a slit in the hammock onto a clean cloth beneath.

Some cultures still practice *couvade*, a custom based on the belief that impending birth affects the father as much as the mother. Some cultures recognize this to the extent that the father too lies in his hammock, abstaining from work, and eating and drinking specific foods for a period of time.

It was the custom of some Caribbean natives to honor a dead chief by placing his body in his hammock and slowly smoking it over a small fire. This is also the practice of the Deni people of Brazil, to keep the body from rotting

during an extended wake. For common people, the Deni and other tribes bury their dead wrapped in a hammock. The Cubeo of Columbia and Brazil bury their dead with a hammock and a calabash gourd. There are similar traditions in Hawaii.

The Kuna of Panama dig a pit or a chamber and place a log or branch across it lengthwise and string a hammock from each end. After placing the body in a hammock, a ceiling is built above the pit and covered with dirt. The Kuna believe the dead sleep in the afterlife, hanging and swinging, as they did in the living world.

IN CEREMONY AND RITUAL
The hammock was developed in cultures where the ordinary and the ceremonial blend into one another. So the hammock is, yes, quite suitable for comfortable sleeping, elevated from the insects,

★ 53

" *'Old Mother.' That is what denizens of the Amazon call their hammocks: As in our first unremembered memories, mae velha enfolds us in comforting arms, besides protecting us from scorpions, mists, and serpents that meander along the ground. The hammock accompanies us like a bed never could through our whole existence. Born in the jungle by the shore of a river, the newborn sleeps his first sleep in the hammock as his grandfather will sleep his last. Then as is our ancient custom, we bury the dead lying down in their own hammock. We are born, we live, we love, we die in the hammock, and then our friends carry us to the boneyard in mae velha to rest up till Judgment Day.* "

—JAMES BOGAN, PROFESSOR AND POET

dampness, and hardness of the ground. And, yes, it can easily be taken down during the daytime. But there are times when the hammock becomes an important part of life transitions.

TRIBAL HAMMOCKS CHANGE

It has only been within the last fifty years that the Central and South American, and particularly Mayan, native hammocks have become a significant import/export item.

They had always been sold to travelers, but the large-scale making and exporting is relatively new.

Different countries and different regions have different styles of hammocks. The Mayans seemed to improve on the early Taino hammocks, which were described as fishnet beds made from tree bark pounded into a rough cord. Taino also made hammocks from woven cotton cloth, the result of their own cotton fields. But the Mayans used a distinctive double or triple weave to make their hammocks. Until the last century, they used a thin cord made from maguey, a palm-like plant in the agave family. The colored cotton string of today's Mayan hammocks is a relatively recent innovation.

The intertwined, sprang-woven pattern is the most distinctive feature of a Mayan hammock. Sprang weaving is one of the oldest weaving methods. It is a very

Many nomadic North American tribes used a folded or gathered blanket as a quick, temporary, and safe baby shelter.

simple, repetitive method of interlocking parallel cords to produce a strong, flat fabric that is fixed in one dimension and expansive in the other dimension. The process does not use a loom and can be done between any vertical posts or small trees. Without the benefit of machinery, it is labor intensive. The bonus of this style, which is also the basis of the Nicaraguan/Central American-style hammock, is that it allows the hammock to contour to the body. The material does not put pressure on the body's pressure points. Instead, weight is evenly distributed, giving a relaxing sensation. Many Mayan hammocks are now made with synthetic fibers, making them stronger and more durable. Cotton, while more comfortable, will not last in any harsh climate if the hammock is used outdoors.

In the small villages of Southeast Mexico,
Mayan descendants continue to teach
their children the Mayan way of weaving.
It takes years to master the craft
and weeks for a skilled artisan
to make one hammock.

THE TRIBAL HISTORY OF HAMMOCKS

In 1890, Scottish anthropologist Sir James Frazer published a lengthy study on mythology and religion in many different cultures of the world. *The Golden Bough* has remained a fascinating literary work and a source of information; it contains several accounts of the use of the hammock:

> *When symptoms of puberty appeared on a girl for the first time, the Guaranis of Southern Brazil, on the borders of Paraguay, used to sew her up in her hammock, leaving only a small opening in it to allow her to breathe. In this condition, wrapt up and shrouded like a corpse, she was kept for two or three days or so long as the symptoms lasted, and during this time she had to observe a most rigorous fast. After that she was entrusted to a matron, who cut the girl's hair and enjoined her to abstain most strictly from eating flesh of any kind until her hair should be grown long enough to hide her ears.*
>
> *In similar circumstances the Chiriguanos of South-eastern Bolivia hoisted the girl in her hammock to the roof, where she stayed for a month: the second month the hammock was let half-way down from the roof; and in the third month old women, armed with sticks, entered the hut and ran about striking everything they met, saying they were hunting the snake that had wounded the girl.*

Amongst the Macusis of British Guiana, when a girl shows the first signs of puberty, she is hung in a hammock at the highest point of the hut. For the first few days she may not leave the hammock by day, but at night she must come down, light a fire, and spend the night beside it, else she would break out in sores on her neck, throat, and other parts of her body. So long as the symptoms are at their height, she must fast rigorously. When they have abated, she may come down and take up her abode in a little compartment that is made for her in the darkest corner of the hut.

Other Indians of Guiana, after keeping the girl in her hammock at the top of the hut for a month, expose her to certain large ants, whose bite is very painful. Sometimes, in addition to being stung with ants, the sufferer has to fast day and night so long as she remains slung up on high in her hammock, so that when she comes down she is reduced to a skeleton.

Brazilian hammocks are made from tightly woven cloth with a brightly colored fringe. They are not as cool as the meshy Mayan hammocks but that's a plus in more temperate areas. Other Central and South American countries and regions also have distinctive hammock characteristics, usually some variation of weave, color, or decoration.

A HAMMOCK BY ANY OTHER NAME

When it was first seen by Spanish and Portuguese explorers in the late 1400s and early 1500s, there were no specific words in Europe for the object. Instead, it was described as being like something else or like a mix of a few other things. So it was referred to as a "bed net" or a "hanging bed." But the name we now know comes from the material from which

some of these hanging beds were made: the bark of the hamac tree, which was pounded and twisted by hand into cord and then woven into this wondrous sleeping and resting device: hamac, hamaca, the hammock.

Even today, as the use of the word "hammock" has spread throughout the world, the names and translations in various languages reflect its lingering, ambiguous, mysterious nature.

"Hamaca" (a thrown fish net)

Dutch = Hangmat
Danish = Hengekøye
English = Hammock
Finnish = Riippumatto
French = Hamac
German = Hangematte
Greek = Kremaste Kounia
Greek (old) = Aiora
Icelandic = Hengirúm
Norwegian = Hengekøye
Portuguese = Rede
Russian = Ga-mák
Spanish = Hamaca
Swedish = Hangmattan
Venezuelan = Chinchorro

Unraveled and laid out,

the threads of a Mayan hammock

measure approximately

two miles in length.

★ 67

Hammocks in the Civilized Home

In the late nineteenth century, hammocks became part of the essential furnishings of the American home. No porch, no yard was complete without its hammock. There was an explosion of variations. Some were made from rich upholstery cloth, simple cheap canvas, or wide, open-weave netting. So the gentle hammock was refined, adapted, souped-up, and just plain messed with.

UNITED STATES PATENT OFFICE.

HERBERT MORLEY SMALL, OF BALDWINSVILLE, MASSACHUSETTS

HAMMOCK.

SPECIFICATION forming part of Letters Patent No 400,131, dated March 26, 1889

Application filed June 10, 1888. Serial No 277,573 (No model)

To all whom it may concern

Be it known that I, HERBERT MORLEY SMALL, of Baldwinsville, in the county of Worcester and State of Massachusetts, have invented a new and Improved Hammock, of which the following is a full, clear, and exact description.

This invention relates to an improvement in hammocks and has special reference to a hammock so constructed that it can be slung from and used with the backs of the seats of ordinary railway passenger-cars.

The invention has for its object to provide a means whereby passengers who are obliged to travel in ordinary passenger-cars at night may be able to sleep with ease and comfort.

The invention consists in a hammock constructed as hereinafter described and claimed.

Reference is to be had to the accompanying drawings forming a part of this specification, in which similar letters of reference indicate corresponding parts in all the figures.

Figure 1 illustrates the invention in use in an ordinary passenger-car. Fig 2 is a view of a hammock constructed in accordance with this invention and Fig 3 represents the end of a hammock provided with a modified form of attachment and legs and feet support.

In carrying out this invention I provide a hammock constructed with the main portion 1 of suitable size and made of netting, canvas, or other suitable material. The main portion 1 is preferably formed of an oblong square shape and curved to form a recess at one end, as at 2, to accommodate the legs of a person hanging over the end. One end of the main portion 1 is provided with hooks 3, adapted to engage the upper edge of the back of a car-seat or other support, and the other curved end is provided with a rope, 4, extending through the eyes 5 of a pair of hooks, 6, adapted to engage the upper edge of the back of a car-seat or other support similar to the first-named hooks 3. By means of this construction the main portion 1 may be swung between the backs of two adjoining car-seats, the hooks 3 hooking over the top edge of the backs of the seats, and the rope 4 extending down through eyes 5 of the hooks and forming a depending loop, the feet of the occupant of the hammock resting in the loop, and the rope 4 moving through the eyes 5 of the hooks to accommodate the loop to the length of the legs hanging over the curved end 2 of the main portion 1.

Instead of the rope 4 forming a single loop it may extend through the eye 5 of a third hook, 6, thereby forming two loops and supports for the feet and legs. The loops of the rope in this case will also accommodate themselves to the length of the legs of the person occupying the hammock, the rope 4 moving through the eyes of the hooks. In this way a comfortable and easy reclining position may be secured and the occupant of the hammock enabled to obtain rest.

Instead of employing the hammock as shown in Fig 1, the occupant may recline practically at full length, by attaching the hooks on the rope 4 to the upper edge of the back of the adjacent seat after the back has been turned over. In this case the rope 4 will have been drawn through the eyes 3 thereby drawing up the loop, and the feet and lower portion of the legs of the occupant of the hammock will rest on the car-seat.

While the invention has been set forth as applied to car-seats, it is obvious that the hammock may be employed in other situations where suitable supports are afforded.

Having thus described my invention, what I claim as new, and desire to secure by Letters Patent, is—

1. A hammock consisting in a seat and back portion, hooks at the upper end of the back portion, a looped rope secured at its ends to the inward corners of the seat portion and adjustable hooks on the parallel parts of the rope, the looped part of the rope forming a foot-rest, substantially as set forth.

2. A hammock constructed with supporting-hooks at one end, and having at its other end a curved recess, and supporting-hooks with a rope passing through eyes in the shanks of the hooks and attached to the corners of the recessed end of the hammock substantially as shown and described.

3. A hammock constructed with main portion 1 having curved recess 2, supporting-hooks 3 at one end and the looped rope 4 with its ends secured at the recessed end of the main portion 1, and the supporting-hooks 6, having eyes 5, through which rope 4 passes, substantially as shown and described.

HERBERT MORLEY SMALL

Witnesses
JOHN R CONANT,
GEO R TUTTLE

(No Model.)

H. M. SMALL.

HAMMOCK.

No. 400,131.   Patented Mar. 26, 1889.

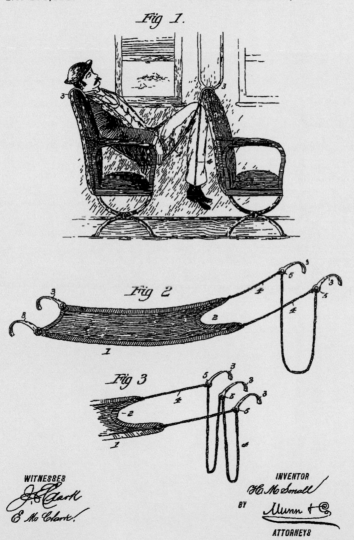

Fig 1.

Fig 2

Fig 3

WITNESSES

J. Clark

E. Mc Clark!

INVENTOR

H. M. Small

BY

Munn & Co.

ATTORNEYS

A hammock obsession began in the early 1880s. In just a three-year period from 1881 to 1883, there were twenty-five different patents granted for changes to the simple hammock. And there were more granted every year: there were special supports, different kinds of coverings, and adaptations of the hammock for all kinds of situations.

Some of the interest in modifying and patenting the hammock may have been that lingering fear: it

"GET THE BEST."
The Flexible Swinging Easy Chair.

(PATENTED MARCH 13, 1883.)

FOR THE

HOUSE, PIAZZA, or LAWN,

The Illustration presents to the eye a recent invention, which is generally conceded to be the **Most Complete, Durable, Simple,** and in every respect, **Perfect Swinging EASY CHAIR** ever brought to the attention of the public. The design is entirely new and original, and it embodies many advantages over such chairs heretofore in use.

It Fits the Form Completely.
Is Perfectly Safe for Children.
No Danger of Falling Out.
Invaluable for Invalids.
A Boon for the Sick and Worn-out.
Can be Used by Several at Once.
The Coolest and Best Made.
Air Circulates Freely while Using.
Is Very Compact when Rolled Up.
Convenient to Carry.

Price, $3.50.

The Children's Flexible Easy Chair

(PATENTED MARCH 7, 1882.)

For the House, Piazza, or Lawn.

The Illustration presents to the eye a recent invention, which is generally conceded to be the **Most Complete, Durable, Simple,** and in every respect, **Perfect Swinging EASY CHAIR** ever brought to the attention of the public. The design is entirely new and original, and it embodies many advantages over such chairs heretofore in use.

It Fits the Form Completely.
Is Perfectly Safe for Children.
No Danger of Falling Out.
Invaluable for Invalids.
A Boon for the Sick and Worn-out.
Can be Used by Several at Once.
The Coolest and Best Made.
Air Circulates Freely while Using.
Is Very Compact when Rolled Up.
Convenient to Carry.

Price, $2.50.

AGENTS WANTED EVERYWHERE.

Manufactured and For Sale by
THE FLEXIBLE HAMMOCK COMPANY
BILLERICA CENTRE, MASS.

Woburn Journal Steam Job Print.

(No Model.)

C. C. TAYLOR.
SUSPENSORY GARMENT.

No. 484,065. Patented Oct. 11, 1892.

Fig. 1. Fig. 2.

74 ★

Fig. 3.

WITNESSES
Gustave Dieterich.
Henry E. Eording.

INVENTOR
Charles C. Taylor
BY
Briesen & Knauth
ATTORNEYS

was just too darn indolent. Changing it, especially making it useful and productive, was a way of converting it. So if you were on a train and you used that special new passenger seat hammock, you could get some rest, arrive fresher than the man next to you, and be ready to work hard. Ah, yes, the hammock actually helps you work better.

But, in all honesty, sometimes a hammock is just a hammock. Many of the designs were simply overwrought versions of the traditional tribal uses. Like the hammock-inspired "suspensory garment." Isn't this just a cloth strap that keeps a child close—similar to the sling that almost all tribal cultures used in some form? In the 1970s we called them "snugglies," a front pack hammock for the newborn.

HAMMOCKS TODAY

There is a popular North American variation, an open weave of cotton rope, called the Pawley's Island Hammock or sometimes the Cape Hatteras Hammock. In addition to weavers in the Carolinas, Virginia-based company Twin Oaks Hammocks has been making hammocks in this style since the late 1960s. They feature wooden spreaders to keep the hammock open and steady.

Another common manufactured version is made from canvas, which also uses wooden spreaders. Such styles are found in catalogs and outdoor furnishing stores and often come with their own hammock stand.

❝*It comes, it goes*—vaivem vaivem. *The oscillation of the hammock is the true enemy of hurry and foe of mindless agitation that demands constant change of scene. Even though the hammock was born in a primeval culture, it can still soothe the rattled body of modern life by reconciling the great contraries of movement and stillness.*❞
—James Bogan, from The Hammock Variations

| # Drafted by Industry

H ammocks became handmaidens to capitalism once they reached industrialized society. They could make parts of the civilized world more efficient and "better."

Beginning in the sixteenth century, the navies of the world embraced the hammock as a way to temporarily use space on the dry gun decks and protect sailors from the damp crowded conditions of the lower decks. The health and morality of the crews immediately improved. Each day the hammocks were "piped up" or "piped down" and when not in use as sleeping quarters, they were rolled and used as extra protection from attack on deck. Even as recently as World War II, sailors inspected

Armies, navies, hospitals, prisons, and orphanages

all embraced the exotic hammock as their own.

their hammocks nightly for bullet damage from the day.

Safety and health might have benefited, but comfort was never an urgent concern.

German mercenaries fighting for the Americans in the Revolutionary War came from Europe by boats on which two men were assigned to each small linen hammock. Diaries are clear about the sleepless nights. In fact, many sailor's diaries are sometimes quite graphic about the atmosphere, sounds, and odors of a hundred or more men bunked in hammocks

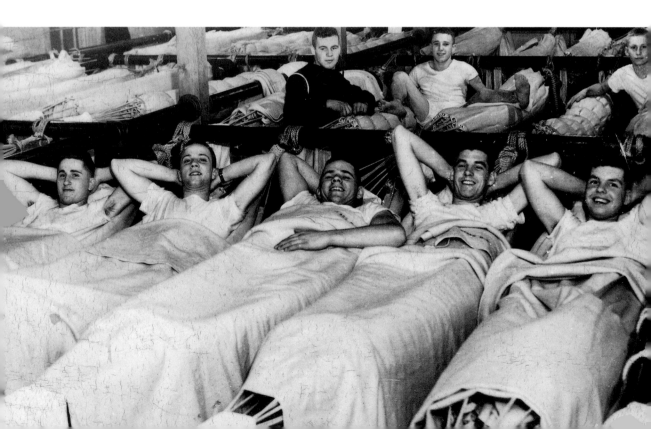

often spaced no more than four-teen inches apart and sometimes suspended six feet in the air.

Armies, too, began using the hammock. It was portable, easy to setup, and kept soldiers off the hard ground away from spiders, insects, snakes, and wetness. In the American Civil War, hammocks were used by both the army and navy, including aboard the early submarine, the USS *Monitor*.

Hammocks became indispens-able as America fought wars in tropi-cal and jungle areas. Teddy Roosevelt used them in the Spanish-American War and a special jungle hammock was developed for World War II and then refined for use in Vietnam.

Prisons, hospitals, and other institutions with transient, unpre-dictable populations all found uses for the hammock. However, the real adaptations were created by independent inventors. Those rest-less pioneers who can never leave well-enough alone were enchanted by the hammock.

The ease and portability of the hammock

made it a favorite for soldiers.

With its cradle-like motion,

the hammock was eventually used

by orphanages across the globe.

At night, missionaries and nurses

often relied on its gentle sway

to soothe whimpering children

under their watch.

THE CARRYING HAMMOCK

It is little surprise that the hammock found a welcoming home with travelers. Its history is tied to nomadic tribes following seasons, crops, and game. The early Taino hammocks were objects of trade that they exchanged with other tribes along the coasts of both Americas.

One minor, but interesting and unusual use of the hammock is as a means of transportation. Very simply, you get in a hammock and two or four men carry you where you are going. Here's a description from the late 1800s from Bishop James Hannington who wrote of his "Peril and Adventure" in Africa for the youth back in England:

There is no more comfortable conveyance in the world than a hammock in Africa. It is slung from a long bamboo pole, overhead a thick awning keeps the sun from the hammock. Across the ends of the pole boards of some three feet long are fastened. The natives wrap a piece of cloth into the

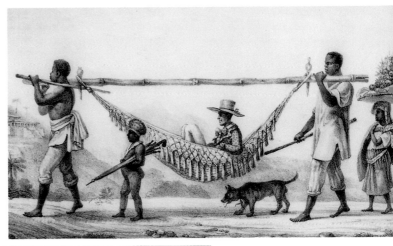

shape of a muffin and place it on their heads, and then take their places, two at each end of the pole, with the ends of the board on their heads. They can trot along at the rate of six miles an hour, for great distances, often keeping up a monotonous song. Their action is perfectly smooth and easy, and the traveler in the hammock, by shutting his eyes, might imagine himself swinging in a cot on board a ship on an almost waveless sea.

Bishop Hannington sounds a bit more forgiving and appreciative than the Cambodian despot Pol Pot, who also traveled through the jungle in a hammock. According to one of his bodyguards, true to his temperament, if he was brushed by even a branch while traveling in the hammock, he would have his carriers beaten.

Carrying hammocks denoted royalty, special persons, and finally tourists. They were part of the charm of traveling on the west coast of the archipelago of Madeira for many years until the early 1960s.

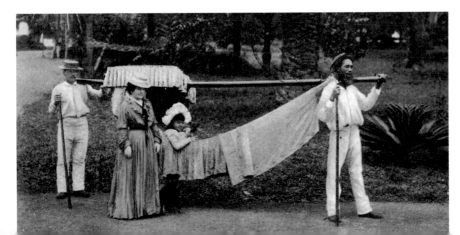

BACKPACKING HAMMOCK

A particular kind of travel, back-packing, has been revolutionized by the hammock. It started when the Army developed the jungle hammock (especially for the Pacific theater) during World War II. It was a smelly, canvas-bottomed, side-zippered, mosquito-netting arrangement that worked pretty well. They were more like portable shelters than simple hammocks. Brave campers and nostalgic veterans bought them up from Army Surplus stores. That's where my father-in-law got the one that went cross-country camping with us in 1978.

Some people know the hammock best through traveling or camping.

★ 95

NATURE'S BEDROOM

Shane Steinkamp started "hammocking" around 1985 in New Orleans, where he works as a software engineer.

To a wanderer, a hammock is more than a simple shelter. It is a feeling. Often, at the end of the day, when it is late and I am tired, cold, hungry, and lonely, I set up my hammock in the firelight. Suddenly a

feeling of comfort comes over me—not just because I have a dry place to sleep, or think that my hammock is cool—but because I am home.

More and more backpackers are discovering hammocks, and with space-age materials and some refinements, hammocks are a sleep system that is comfortable, lightweight, and easy to use. . . . More important than the technological revolution among backpackers, however, is the philosophical revolution. A tent is a struggle against nature. Heavy pads must be carried to cushion soft bodies from hard ground, and there is always some trade-off between comfort and weight. A level place must be found. Rocks. sticks, fir cones, and other discomforts must be cleared and natural elements disturbed. The tent is then erected as a portable fortress against nature, and even after the backpacker moves on, the cleared space and crushed vegetation are a persistent sign of his passage.

A hammocker, however, does not struggle against nature. No level place is needed, and rocks, roots, thorns, poison ivy, and the little critters of nature are not a concern. A hammock can be used where no traditional tent or tarp can, and a hammocker will never be stuck sleeping on the tortuous blasphemy of a wooden tent platform.

With a good hammock and a few essentials in a backpack, a hiker becomes a sojourner in nature. The entire wood is his bedroom, and anywhere he cares to hang his bed becomes his camp for the night. In the morning, he packs back up and walks away, leaving nothing but footprints and two trees who will tell the story about how they helped a friend by each holding an end of his bed for a few hours while he got some rest. "Much better than those dirt campers rolling around on the ground and snoring all night!" one will say. "Harrumph! Indeed, indeed, my brother. Why, it makes me wish I could lay down and have a nap!"

The growing interest
in outdoor living
includes a
curiousity about
outdoor sleeping.

NATURE'S INSPIRATION

Man gets all the credit for inventing the hammock, but it was clearly Mother Nature who inspired him. One need only observe and appreciate the outdoors to notice the hammocklike patterns repeated amongst earth's fauna and flora.

One sees a hammock in the nests birds make to lay their eggs and the hives bees build to protect their honey. It's seen in the way the kangaroo keeps her joey warm and safe in her pouch, and in the way the pelican uses her deep beak to both scoop fish from the sea and to cradle her chicks. Just as fishermen cast their nets, spiders sew webs to catch their prey. The hammock, simplistic in its function and form, parallels with nature so beautifully.

★ 101

chapter 4

The Troublesome Hammock

The hammock is a seditious item. It's soft and inviting—and therein lies the problem.

The hammock flies in the face of one of the most precious and treasured canons of the industrial world: the hammock is not about work—it's about not work. That's troublesome in a culture built on what has been called the Protestant Leisure Ethic: that it's okay to not be working just so long as you are still productive and competitive.

Tell me if I'm wrong. The more leisure resembles work, the easier it is to fit into our lives. We have learned that working is morally superior to just plain leisure. Acceptable leisure is "productive" and results in projects, achievements, rewards, and winning.

The hammock has the ability to untie the bonds, not only to work itself—our job, our workday—but it actually works on our attitudes toward life.

THAT

DIABOLICAL

HAMMOCK

1. " Where Shall I Hang It ? "

2. " That's About the Right Height "

3. " Ugh ! How It Stretches ! "

4. " Hope that Knot Won't Slip "

5. The Ascent

6. The Descent

7. Capital Thing for Preserving the Strawberries

8. " The Church Bells are Ringing, Jamie "

We all carry that little tension in us as we approach the hammock. "Do I remember how to get into this thing? Is this hammock different from other hammocks? Will I be able to get out . . . with grace? Should I really be doing this at all? Oh, I forgot my book—and something to drink. Someone's going to say something if they see me just lying here. There are better things to do. This is for the kids." Shall I go on?

Once you do get into the hammock, you probably develop a form of "Hammock Face." One such expression is a slightly large, almost theatrical grin, one that borders on pain. "Yes, this is fine, just fine." It seems related to the pain and pleasure of a good teeth cleaning.

The second most common expression is "I'm resting." It's a look of studied meditation as you lie there, still, with arms folded. Sometimes you look like you're sleeping . . . or dead.

The Hammock Face has been around ever since the hammock showed up in the backyards, front yards, porches, and side yards of the industrial world.

The End Result

Once you get over the basic novelty of the hammock, a new world opens up. The friendly cradling of the hammock is unique in the world of furniture. No matter how much ergonomic engineering goes into a chair, there are still hard edge materials creating the shape. So the holding aspect of a hammock is quite a wonderful thing.

Then there's the organic nature of the hammock. It begins most simply with one's suspension in the air: you achieve a floating sensation, like a leaf. There are a few birds' nests that have a hammocklike quality.

Then there's the movement: the rocking, the swinging. It can be fast or slow; it can pick up tempo or slow down to a near nodding. That is a primitive, comforting feeling that none of us has really forgotten. Our bodies are mostly water and that movement is the tidal, maybe amniotic sloshing, the memory of which runs deep.

chapter 5

Caring for Your Hammock

HANGING A HAMMOCK

The first thing to look for when hanging a hammock is a pair of hardwood trees, a foot or more in diameter, with no rotting. If you opt to hang your hammock from posts, plant them at least two feet in the ground, fill the hole with cement, and let dry for three days (longer if it is particularly humid or rainy). For a traditional rope hammock with spreader bars, the minimum distance between trees or posts should be equal to the total length of the hammock. If the trees are further apart than the total length of the hammock, you will need to use rope or chain to extend the hanging points of your hammock. The height you hang the hammock from depends on personal taste and the hammock itself, though

The proper care, cleaning, and storage of your hammock will add years to its life.

about four feet from the ground is a good rule of thumb. Consider asking a friend or family member to sit in the hammock as you test different heights.

A hammock without spreader bars, or a Mayan hammock, has more leeway with the hanging distance between trees or posts. In this case, the distance should be less than the total length of the hammock, as these types of hammocks are meant to maintain a comfortable curve. An ideal distance is about two-thirds of the overall length of the hammock, again adjusting for personal preference and the individual hammock.

Cleaning a Hammock

Always clean your hammock thoroughly before storing it for winter. You can spot clean your hammock at any time, but an annual scrubbing with cool soapy water will add years to the life of your hammock. Pick a day with no rain in the forecast; your hammock will likely need

a few days in the sun to dry completely. To begin, take down your hammock and place it on a clean, hard surface. In a large bucket, combine about a cup of mild detergent with a couple gallons of water. Using a soft bristle brush (even a bristle hairbrush will do), gently clean the hammock on both sides, being careful not to snag the weave. After cleaning, rinse the hammock using a garden hose and hang it in direct sunlight to dry. Handle your hammock with extra care while the fabric is still damp. Don't lift a wet hammock by its ends as it may stretch and lose its shape.

STORING A HAMMOCK

It is important to remove your hammock during the winter months to avoid needless moisture and wear. (It is also advisable to remove your hammock during any severe storms during the months it is in use and hang it when the rain clears.) Before

★ 113

storing your hammock, make sure it is clean and completely dry. Fold the hammock in half by bringing the hanging rings together. Place it in a large, breathable, waterproof bag and store in a garage or other dry place protected from the elements and vermin. Alternately, the hammock can be hung by its rings in a dry, indoor area such as a basement or closet.

ENCHANTED KNOTS

BY MINDA NOVEK, WRITER, BROOKLYN, NEW YORK

In a heap, my hammock looks deceptively simple, a small pile of threads spilled on the floor. But when hung in its proper place—between two poles, or trees or even the hooks I've drilled into various New York apartment walls—it takes on the practical yet magical properties of a genie in a bottle, responsive to my immediate desires. As a portable form of bliss, my hammock has traveled with me to many places and served many functions. Blue as a Caribbean sky and finely wrought as a spider's web, it has weathered through thirty-plus years of use in a Vermont art colony, an upstate New York retreat, a SoHo loft, an inner city children's center backyard, and more. Hammocks were once used for low impact transport, but even when staying put, they take you someplace new. Mine has been as neutral or engaging an environment as needed, a place to sleep, read, eat, or brainstorm in; a restful cocoon, a playground swing, a gentle, recuperative sling, a love nest, an ocean, a womb. It is the oasis I enter when all around me seems too weighty or arid, softening the gravity of life into a floating smile.

| # Loosen the Knots

GOOD FOR THE BACK?

Back pain is the number two reason Americans visit their physicians. Eighty percent of us will at some point be afflicted by it, and the number of treatments is numerous. Listed amongst them are physical therapy, massage, acupuncture, and yes, even sleeping in a Mayan hammock.

Not all doctors are convinced, but there are patients that swear by it. The theory suggests that the Mayan hammock allows the back to find its natural alignment. Without the pressure applied by traditional mattresses, muscles can supposedly release pent-up tension. These claims aren't completely without merit. *The Journal of the American Medical Association* once

This rustic, swinging log raft is a kind of playful, but not too restful hammock.

boasted in an article that the Mayan hammock offers exceptional back support.

Before personally putting this theory to the test, remember that not all hammocks are created equal. The Mayan hammock has some unique features—there is no stretcher bar; the fabric is made of a tight, meshlike weave; and they're designed to be slept in perpendicularly, not vertically. It is also important that both sides of the hammock are hung equal distances from the ground. Otherwise, you'll miss out on the benefit of having all your body weight equally distributed.

A Place of Meditation

While resort shopping for your next Caribbean vacation you may find that some of them are offering "hammock meditation."

Buddhist monks have long used their hammocks as a peace-ful place to meditate, and it's not hard to understand why. Hammocks can aid in the illusion of weightlessness, a desired sensation

in meditation and a welcomed contrast to a thin yoga mat on a hardwood floor. Some yogis have even begun incorporating the hammock into their practice. The soft woven seat of the hammock offers a comfortable spot for breathing exercises and some seated poses.

The hammock is a universal symbol for rest and relaxation.

See one in your dreams and it's often a sign that you're in need of a vacation.

Nantucket Hammock

THE
MOST COMPLETE
HAMMOCK
In Existence

Can be completely enclosed with extra awnings for outdoor sleeping

For veranda; requires space only six feet long and may be hoisted, cushions and all, SNUG against ceiling when not in use. Made of heavy ducks and denims, any color, reinforced, trimmed with white binding, or can be had in awning stripe; cushions and pillows are filled with fibre made from non-absorbent pine needles. Fitted with ropes, pulleys, deck cleats and galvanized snaps exactly the same as used on rigging of first-class yachts.

Complete with Cushions and Rigging, ready to hang , $18-20-22-27
Frame and Adjustable Canopy for lawn . . . . . . $15.00 extra
Combination Tent Curtains to entirely enclose Hammock, 10.00 "

Send for descriptive pamphlet and samples. Address Dept. E

BICKFORD BROS., ROCHESTER, N. Y.
Child's Lawn Tent, fancy stripe, $12.00

The Eagleston Hammock

THE NEWEST AND BEST

Made from heavy brown or grey canvas. Mattresses covered with blue, green or red denim. Note pockets in end for magazines and papers. For price and circulars address

Department 20,

THE EAGLESTON SHOP

Hyannis   Massachusett

PALMER'S HAMMOCKS

AWARDED TWENTY TWO MEDALS

SEND FOR FREE BOOKLET

PALMER'S HAMMOCKS are strong and graceful. They retain their shape and color and do not snap the cords.
PALMER'S HAMMOCKS are for sale by all the leading dealers — ask for them. We are pioneers in the business and have the largest plant of the kind in the world.

I. E. PALMER
Send for a copy of our FREE BOOKLET "C." It explains just what you should know about hammocks.
Middletown, Conn.

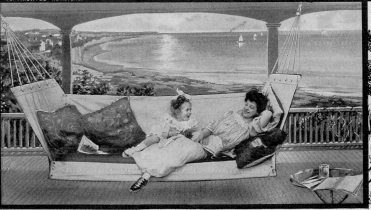

GLOUCESTER SWINGING BED HAMMOCK

COPYRIGHTED REGISTERED

For Porches, Lawns, Tents, Bungalows, Dens—Combines Hammock, Couch and Swing Seat

The Gloucester Swinging Bed Hammock occupies no more room than the ordinary hammock, but utilizes it all; there are fifteen square feet of available space in this hammock—it does not waste room as the ordinary hammock does.

In this hammock you can stretch out full length, freely and at ease, with none of the cramped, doubled up position that one must assume in the ordinary hammock, and there is no netting to catch in the clothing or wrap around the neck. The canvas ends make comfortable back and head rests.

There is plenty of room in it

for the children to play with their toys or for the mother to sit with her sewing. When callers come it helps out the seating capacity of the porch, for it is large enough and strong enough to seat half a dozen people at once.

By means of the Gloucester Swinging Bed Hammock any porch or balcony may be readily converted into an outdoor sleeping room.

May be used indoors

The Gloucester Swinging Bed Hammock is a fine thing for the children to play in, keeping them off the floor, which is apt to be cold and draughty in winter.

The Gloucester Hammock makes a very decorative and appropriate piece of furniture for dens and bungalows, particularly where an outdoor or marine effect is desired.

Although but recently put upon the market, the Gloucester Hammock was made by the head of our house as far back as 1870 from the model used by the officers of the United States Navy.

It is made of heavy canvas

and will last a lifetime. Furthermore, with the mattress removed, the hammock is weather-proof and may be left out in the rain without damage.

The frame of the Gloucester Hammock is strongly constructed of seasoned wood, and the fittings are made of heavy galvanized iron. It has a thick mattress with removable mattress cover.

It can be hoisted to ceiling when not in use. It is made without or with wind shields as shown in picture. Carefully covered and packed with lines and hooks ready for hanging, and sent anywhere by express or freight.

Write for Descriptive Booklet

telling more about the advantages and uses of this hammock, and price list of styles and sizes. The genuine Gloucester Hammock is sold only direct by us, the makers. Write us to-day for particulars—hammock weather is due.

E. L. ROWE & SON, Inc., 32 Wharf Street, GLOUCESTER, MASS.

The simple hammock—that cousin of the fishing net—keeps changing with every culture it encounters.

So, find a hammock. Spend more time in it than you think you should.

See what happens.

★ ACKNOWLEDGMENTS ★

This book is a hammock. The threads are many. Of course, the people who first devised a way to cool and rest in such a way! And the people today whose lives are crisscrossed with the hammock: those makers around the world. Then there are those of us who are in awe of the hammock: James Bogan, Tom Hennessey, Ed Speer, Shane Steinkamp, the late Denison Andrews, and John Watson. Thank you to photo researcher and hammock lover, Minda Novek, and poets Li-Young Lee and Kate Gale. Thank you photo archivist Scott Bilotta and agent Scott Mendel who first said the word "hammock" to me. Finally, thank you to editors Marisa Bulzone and Kristen Latta at Stewart, Tabori & Chang, and book designer, Anna Christian.

Photographs are courtesy of the following people and collections: Keith Levit: pages 2-3; Todd Taulman: 5; Courtesy of Scott Bilotta: 6, 7, 10, 27, 39, 68, 69, 98-99; Adam Johnson: 9; ChipPix: 12; Rhett Stansbury: 16-17; Peter Elvidge: 18; Fosh: 19; Chicago History Museum, *Chicago Daily News*, DN-0074328B: 21; Ashley Hockenberry: 22; Magdalena Bujak: 23; Jose Marines: 24-25; Imke Schulze: 26; Bradley Mason: 27; Shutterstock: 28; Garrett Scott: 29; Jaime Monfort Arjona: 29; Fredrik Schjold: 29; Shawn Hoon: 29; Ingret: 30; Mark Graves: 31; Christopher Russo: 32; James Balzano, Jr.: 35; Cliché G. Kante: 36; Library of Congress, USF34-031272-D: 37; Tribal Photo: 40; Tricia Tan: 43; David S. April: 45; Library of Congress, USZ62-53665: 46; Library of Congress, USZ62-65346: 47; Tribal Photo: 50; Library of Congress, USZ62-77108: 51; Library of Congress, USZ62-77110: 52; Smithsonian Institution, National Anthropological Archives: 53; Yale Collection of Western Americana, Beinecke Rare Book and Manuscript Library: 54, 55; Mayan Legacy: 56, 57; Diana Mary Jorgenson: 58-59; Germaine Walter Bora, Courtesy of Vixctor Quispe: 61; Jesus Parazo: 62; Galen R. Frysinger: 63; James M. Phelps, Jr.: 64; Vitaly Chernyshenko: 64; Dario Diament: 65; Alex James Bramwell: 66-67; Kyle Tremlett: 75; Nicole Weiss: 76; Liz Persun: 77; Joy Brown: 79; Canada Deptartment of National Defence, Library and Archives Canada, PA-104184: 81; Chicago History Museum, *Chicago Daily News*, DN-0005126: 86; Chicago History Museum, *Chicago Daily News*, DN-0001423: 87; Library of Congress, USZ62-62806: 89; M. De la Bouglise, Library and Archives Canada, PA-164763: 89; New Tribe, Inc.: 92, 94, 95; Muriel Lasure: 93; Kenneth Chelette: 96; Dan Bannister: 100; Andrey Grinyov: 100; Lori Skelton: 101; Jennifer Driscoll: 101; Mark Koenig: 101; Mihail Orlov: 101; Sandra O'Claire: 106; Dragan Trifunovic: 108; Tony Strong: 111; Katja Kodba: 112; Tomasz Otap: 113; Jonathan Feinstein: 115; WizData, Inc.: 117; Shutterstock: 118-119; Dario Diament: 120; Adely Adnan: 121; Dennis Sabo: 124-125; Ewa Brozek: 126

Published in 2008 by Stewart, Tabori & Chang, an imprint of Harry N. Abrams, Inc.

Text copyright © 2008 by Daniel Mack

Library of Congress Cataloging-in-Publication Data:
Mack, Daniel.   The hammock: a celebration of a summer classic / Daniel Mack.   p. cm.
ISBN-13: 978-1-58479-574-2   ISBN-10: 1-58479-574-3
1. Hammocks. I. Title.   TS1781.M23 2007   684.1'8—dc22

Editors: Marisa Bulzone and Kristen Latta   Designer: Anna Christian   Production Manager: Tina Cameron

The text of this book was composed in Adobe Garamond.

Printed and bound in China
10 9 8 7 6 5 4 3 2 1

HNA
harry n. abrams, inc.
a subsidiary of La Martinière Groupe
115 West 18th Street
New York, NY 10011
www.hnabooks.com